C000228424

LAM
BISHOP'
LLAWHAD

CARSWELL MEDIEVAL HOUSE
CAREW CROSS

Rick Turner MA, FSA

Contents

A TOUR IN SOUTH PEMBROKESHIRE	2
THE HISTORICAL BACKGROUND	4
A HISTORY OF LAMPHEY PALACE	7
A TOUR OF LAMPHEY PALACE	15
A HISTORY OF LLAWHADEN CASTLE	29
A TOUR OF LLAWHADEN CASTLE	35
CARSWELL MEDIEVAL HOUSE	45
A History of the House	45
A Description of the House	45
The Dating and Function of the House	47
CAREW CROSS	49
The Inscription	50
Later History of the Cross	51
FEATURES	
Lamphey Palace: The Development of the Buildings	12
The Painted Decoration at Lamphey Palace	17
A Bird's-Eye View of Lamphey Palace	26
Llawhaden Castle: The Development of the Buildings	32
A Bird's-Eye View of Llawhaden Castle	37
A Tour of the Borough of Llawhaden	43
Further Reading	52

Series Editor David M. Robinson *BSc, PhD, FSA*
Designed by Icon Design

First Published 1991; Second Edition (Revised) 2000

© *Cadw: Welsh Historic Monuments (Crown Copyright),*
Crown Building, Cathays Park, Cardiff, CF10 3NQ.

Printed in Great Britain by South Western Printers

ISBN 1 85760 111 4

A late eighteenth-century watercolour by John 'Warwick' Smith (1749–1831), showing Lamphey Bishop's Palace as an ivy-clad ruin (National Library of Wales, PD 9341).

A TOUR IN SOUTH PEMBROKESHIRE

Lying in the beautiful south Pembrokeshire countryside, perhaps a little in the shadow of the celebrated medieval castles at Carew and Pembroke, there is a small but no less significant group of historic monuments which together form the subject of this guide. When compared to their famous neighbours, the sites are not especially well known, though each is certainly worthy of our attention in its own right.

The two largest monuments, the bishop's palace at Lamphey and the castle at Llawhaden, represent the ruins of once major residences belonging to the powerful medieval bishops of St Davids. At Carswell, on the other hand, the visitor will find no more than a modest stone dwelling, the comparatively rare survival of a yeoman's house from the later Middle Ages. Finally, the superb early Christian carved and inscribed cross near the gates of Carew Castle is a powerful and vibrant reminder of the pre-Conquest kingship of Deheubarth, in the years before the Norman invasion of this region created the so-called 'little England beyond Wales'.

All four sites are now in the care of Cadw: Welsh Historic Monuments. Indeed, the wheel-head of the Carew Cross provides the inspiration for the distinctive emblem or symbol which currently represents the organization. Should you wish to look at any one particular monument, the guide is arranged on an individual site basis. However, all four monuments lie within 12 miles (19.3km) of one another, and — if you have the time — they can easily be explored as part of a fascinating day's tour.

Left: *The medieval bishops of St Davids bore great temporal as well as spiritual power, holding several major estates including those centred on Lamphey Palace and Llawhaden Castle. This late thirteenth-century manuscript illustration shows archbishops and a group of clergy (British Library, Cotton Vitellius Ms. A XIII, f. 6v).*

Right: *Dramatically sited in the south Pembrokeshire countryside, Llawhaden was to become the richest estate held by the medieval bishops of St Davids. The initial fortification of the Norman period was developed to serve as a comfortable residence at the centre of the manorial estate (Skyscan Balloon Photography, for Cadw: Welsh Historic Monuments).*

THE HISTORICAL BACKGROUND

Lamphey Palace and Llawhaden Castle were, by any standards, fairly major medieval episcopal residences, and are the two most prominent monuments covered in this guide. In considering the details and significance of both sites, it is important for us to appreciate that medieval bishops — including those of St Davids — spent much of their lives on the move. It was, for example, necessary to tour their diocese from time to time on a wide variety of spiritual matters. Much effort was also spent in visiting their extensive estates to ensure their proper management, as well as to consume the food they produced. Moreover, such powerful prelates were required to spend a considerable amount of time in London, attending the royal court and Parliament. In all, these men had great temporal authority as well as religious power and influence, often becoming bishops, not just by service to the church, but more importantly through service to the king.

To house himself and his considerable retinue, both in the cathedral city and when on the move, a bishop needed a number of great houses. As early as the twelfth century, for example, the bishops of Winchester administered their enormous estates from eight principal locations: six castles and two palaces. Yet more remarkable were the archbishops of Canterbury, who — at one time — had up to twenty-one palaces to choose from. In such a pattern of ownership, the bishops of St Davids were no exception.

Throughout the diocese, especially at the centre of significant land holdings, the medieval bishops gradually acquired a variety of manorial, fortified, and often quite palatial buildings, all of which required considerable funds for their regular maintenance and upkeep. Apart from Lamphey and Llawhaden, the bishops of St Davids also possessed a palace in the tiny cathedral city itself. This truly magnificent building (which is also in the care

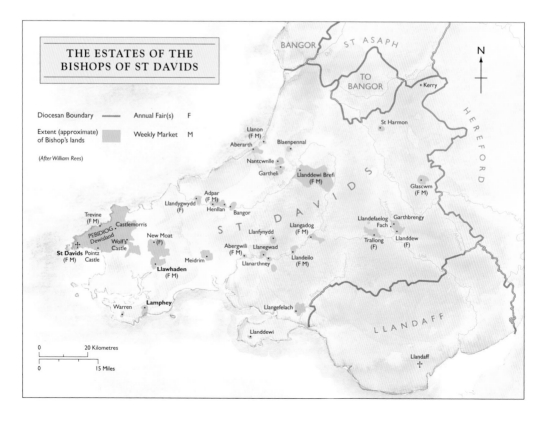

Although the bishops of St Davids held a number of manorial and palatial buildings throughout the diocese, it was the residence at St Davids that was always referred to as Palatium, *the palace par excellence (Skyscan Balloon Photography, for Cadw: Welsh Historic Monuments).*

The seal of Bishop Henry de Gower (1328–47), perhaps the greatest of the medieval builder–bishops of St Davids (Society of Antiquaries).

of Cadw) is situated alongside the cathedral church of St Andrew and St David. It was almost completely rebuilt during the time of Bishop Henry de Gower (1328–47). Other residences are known to have been maintained at various times at Llanddew, Llanddewi, Llandygwydd, New Moat, Trevine and Wolf's Castle. Outside the diocese, the bishops had an 'inn' or great house in London. By 1301, this 'inn' was located off Fleet Street, near St Bride's church, close to the site where King Henry VIII (1509–47) eventually built his palace of Bridewell.

By 1342, such was the expense of constant upkeep at all of these sites, that Bishop Henry de Gower decided to retain and keep in repair only seven of the palaces and manor houses on his Welsh estates. It appears that the others were gradually left to fall into ruin.

Lamphey Palace and Llawhaden Castle, together with the palaces at Trevine and especially St Davids, were always among the more significant sites, and the focus of the most lavish building programmes undertaken by the medieval bishops. Each one, however, must have looked quite different in its prime, and certainly they had very different histories. Even so, they are united in terms of overall function. More than anything else, the differences reflected changes in fashion and personal taste, as successive bishops sought to adapt the work of their predecessors to their own particular needs and preferences.

Turning to the two smaller monuments covered in the guide, the old house at Carswell is an example of a medieval dwelling peculiar to southern Pembrokeshire. In his *Description of Pembrokeshire*, written as early as 1603, George Owen said '*The masons were so skillful in ould tyme that in these counties most Castells and houses of any accompt were builded with vaultes very stronglie ...*'. Indeed, this is true of Lamphey and Llawhaden, as well as Carswell. Essentially, such first-floor dwellings with vaulted undercrofts are seen as residences of the wealthier upper classes. And, despite its small size, Carswell represents the home of a fairly prosperous yeoman farmer. It is rare for such a building to have survived with so little alteration into modern times.

The last of the monuments in the guide is the oldest. The Carew Cross was probably erected about 1035 as a memorial to the native Welsh prince, Maredudd ap Edwin of Deheubarth, great-grandson of the famous Welsh 'law-maker', Hywel Dda (d. 949/50). It is one of more than 400 sculptured slabs and crosses, dating from the fifth to eleventh centuries, which are loosely grouped as the early Christian monuments of Wales. Carew is one of the later examples, and is undoubtedly one of the finest. Its rich carving and intricate patterns betray both native and Viking influences.

A HISTORY OF LAMPHEY PALACE

BEFORE THE BLACK BOOK

The early history of Lamphey remains unclear. The place name is derived from the Welsh, Llandyfái, 'the church of Tyfái'. According to the twelfth-century life of St Teilo, given in the *Book of Llandaff*, Tyfái was a nephew of the great Teilo. The life tells how Tyfái was killed whilst still an infant, trying to protect a swineherd from a ruthless magnate named Tutic. Lamphey *may* have been one of the estates granted to the monastery of Teilo at Penally — the place where Tyfái was buried. It was perhaps the gift of the local king, Aircol Lawhir, granted in recompense for the cruel deed.

There is, however, much confusion in the complex source for this story. The theme is a familiar one. Clearly, the burial of Tyfái at Penally was an event of some importance, and was eventually the basis for consolidating a landed estate. In turn, the detail from the life of Teilo may represent justification for a claim on the estate by the bishop of Llandaff (the church of St Teilo) at the expense of the early medieval bishops of St Davids.

Whatever the truth of the pre-Conquest ownership of Lamphey, by the time of the Norman invasion, it was clearly part of the estates of the bishops of St Davids and was to remain so until the reign of King Henry VIII. The earliest reference to a bishop's residence here is indicated in a story related by Gerald of Wales (d. 1223). In 1096, the Normans were under siege by the Welsh in the newly constructed castle and town at Pembroke. As the scholar–cleric tells us, in an effort to fool the besiegers about the lack of food in the town, the Norman leader, Gerald of Windsor, sent letters to his lord, Arnulf of Montgomery, saying that his provisions would be sufficient for the next four months. The letters fell into the hands of Bishop Wilfred (1085–1115) — just as the cunning Gerald had intended. In turn the bishop passed them on to the Welsh leaders, who were discouraged and abandoned their siege. In fact, Pembroke

was never retaken from the Normans. At the time, the bishop was living at a house 'hard by' — a location which may well have been Lamphey.

Wilfred's actions may have contributed, in part, to the decisions taken on his death in 1115. The bishopric of St Davids, together with its considerable estates, were transferred to a Norman, Bernard (1115–48), former chaplain to Henry I's queen, Matilda (d. 1118). From then on this important diocese and all of its episcopal possessions passed under the authority of the archbishops of Canterbury and, indirectly, were in the control of the king of England.

Nothing is known of the original palace at Lamphey, though it seems likely that the buildings would have been of timber. The earliest surviving remains appear to date from the early thirteenth century. In 1210–12, Gerald of Wales wrote to Bishop Geoffrey de Henlaw (1203–14) accusing him of burdening the priests of Carew, Stackpole and Tenby by staying with them with his retinue, when this was unnecessary given the proximity of his manor of Lamphey.

The building of the fine new western hall, probably by Bishop Richard Carew (1256–80), is unfortunately unrecorded in any surviving document. In 1290, Bishop Thomas Bek (1280–93) was granted licence to hold an annual four-day fair at Lamphey, and in 1291 he was given free warren (the right to keep rabbits) of the manor.

Far Left: The palace at Lamphey overlooks the site of medieval fishponds, now overgrown with reeds. To the left are the partially hidden remains of the western hall, probably built by Bishop Richard Carew (1256–80). To the right, you can just glimpse the distinctive arcaded parapet of Bishop Henry de Gower's hall.

Left: The seal of Bishop Richard Carew, who was probably responsible for building the western hall at Lamphey (The Vatican Archives, A. A. Arm. I–XVIII, 2190, 11).

The Black Book *paints a picture of a well-run estate at Lamphey, with a rich agricultural economy. This near-contemporary manuscript illustration from the* Lutrell Psalter *shows a grain harvest in progress; the produce from such activity was no doubt stored in the bishop's great barn (British Library, Additional Ms. 42130, f. 172v).*

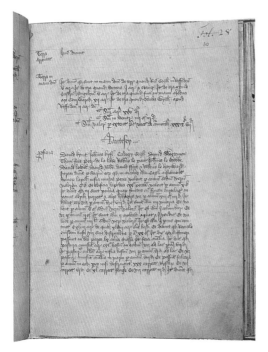

The Black Book of St Davids *was compiled in 1326 for Bishop David Martin (1293–1328). It was a detailed survey of all the lands and estates held by the bishop and was kept for centuries as a source of reference. The surviving early sixteenth-century copy yields much information on the richness of the Lamphey estate. This folio shows the opening of the Lamphey entry (British Library, Additional Ms. 34125, f. 30).*

THE BLACK BOOK AND THE LATER MIDDLE AGES

A full and very revealing account of the Lamphey estate around this time comes from a detailed survey of the lands of the bishops of St Davids taken in 1326 — the so-called *Black Book of St Davids*. The survey refers to the palace as 'the stone houses within the walls of the gate', whose value was the equivalent of £5 per annum. There were further stone buildings outside the gate, worth 10*s.* per annum, together with two watermills and a windmill. Also included were three orchards which produced apples, cabbages, leeks and other produce. There were four fishponds and a dovecot, to provide fish and meat, and there was a park containing 144 customary acres (perhaps 170 statute acres; 68.8ha), of which 48 acres were woodland. The park was managed to produce a range of crops: underwood or coppice wood for fuel and craft goods, rushes for thatching or floor covering, ferns for the bedding of animals or the making of potash, and peat for fuel. The park also contained 'sixty great beasts, as well as the wild animals'. The great beasts were horses and cattle, and the wild animals probably included deer, hares and rabbits. Today, the remains of a small medieval tower house survive in the middle of the park — the dwelling used by the park-keeper or 'parker'. In all, the *Black Book* paints a picture of a very rich and well-tended estate around which was the largest manor in the bishop's holding with 427 acres (173ha) of arable land.

The tenants of this manor owed the bishop a surprising range of feudal duties and agricultural services. They had to fight in his army if so required, transport building materials and coal for burning lime, repair mills and transport the millstones. On their deaths, tenants had to forfeit their best horse or suit of clothes, depending on their wealth. They even had to take their bread to be baked at Llawhaden or Burton. A special duty was to load the bishop's wagons with wine at Carew, Pembroke, or Tenby and to convey it safely to the lord's cellar, where they were to rack it, all at their own cost. For all this, the tenants had the right to sit in the bishop's hall, 'at the tablecloth'.

There was renewed building at the palace during the episcopate of Bishop Henry de Gower (1328–47), but the Black Death of 1348–49 must have taken a heavy toll on the population of Lamphey, and there is evidence that agricultural production was seriously cut back.

Over the next century and a half, the episcopal registers show that from time to time the bishops continued to use Lamphey for accommodation. Indeed, when they were in the diocese, it appears to have been their most favoured residence. With the bishop present, the palace would become the centre of administration for the whole see of St Davids.

In 1486, for example, the palace chapel was the scene of the interrogation of Roger Burley, a chaplain in Pembroke, on a charge of heresy. Soon after this time, probably before 1510, the western hall was remodelled. Then, in 1507, Bishop Robert Sherborne (1505–08) played host to the great Sir Rhys ap Thomas (d. 1525). The bishop blessed Sir Rhys and all the combatants who had come from across Wales to take part in the celebrated tournament held at Carew Castle. In turn, Sherborne was succeeded as bishop by Edward Vaughan (1509–22). Lamphey was apparently Vaughan's favourite manor, and the antiquary John Leland (writing in the 1530s) tells us that he was responsible for rebuilding the chapel and building a great garner or barn.

Another very accurate picture of Lamphey is given in an inventory of the palace and its grounds taken on the death of Bishop Richard Rawlins in 1536. There were twenty-seven rooms mentioned and by far the most richly furnished, decorated with hangings and carpets, was the bishop's own chamber, whose contents were worth the vast sum of £157 7s. 10d. In contrast, the contents of the hall and parlour were worth £1 10s. and £1 18s. 2d. respectively. There were seven other main chambers for the bishop's guests, and rooms for the servants who included a cook, porter, barber and brewer.

Above: *The seal of Bishop Richard Rawlins (1523–36) on whose death an extensive inventory was made of the palace and its grounds. Of the twenty-seven rooms mentioned, it records that the bishop's own chamber was the most richly furnished (Public Record Office, E 25/84, pt 1).*

Lamphey continued to be a favoured residence of the bishops of St Davids in the years after the Black Death (1348–49). The remodelling of the western hall in the early sixteenth century provided for the entertaining of the spiritually and temporally powerful. This detail from a late fifteenth-century manuscript shows a group of bishops preparing to dine in style with their royal host (British Library, Royal Ms. 14 E IV, f. 244v).

There were also rooms for the storage and preparation of food, including the wine cellar, which contained all the silver, together with five hogsheads of claret and one of white wine. The bishop had a large library covering divinity, the humanities, philosophy, medicine and law. In the palace precinct were ancillary buildings such as the fish larder, brewhouse and bakehouse, and in the grounds there were three pairs of swans and a pair of peacocks.

Bishop Rawlin's successor, Bishop William Barlow (1536–48), a somewhat arrogant and tactless man, chose to neglect the Pembrokeshire possessions of his see and sought to move the cathedral from St Davids to Carmarthen. It was Barlow who in August 1546 decided — or was perhaps forced — to surrender his richest manor of Lamphey to King Henry VIII, in return for the quite valuable rectory of Carew. It should be said that Barlow was not alone in losing one of his episcopal palaces at this time, for some 65 from a total of 176 such residences were appropriated by the Crown during the reigns of Henry VIII and Elizabeth I (1558–1603).

LATER HISTORY

In October 1546 the manor was granted to Richard Devereux (d. 1547) and, despite the efforts of Bishop Robert Ferrar (1548–55) to recover it, Lamphey remained in the hands of the influential Devereux family for the next century. Richard's son, Walter (d. 1576), who was created first earl of Essex in 1572, must have spent some of his childhood and adult life at the palace. In turn, he passed the estate at Lamphey on to his brother, George, who lived there between 1576 and 1597. The palace is also associated with Walter's son, Robert — the second earl of Essex and flamboyant favourite of the ageing Queen Elizabeth — whose career ended with his execution on Tower Hill on a charge of high treason in 1601. However, between graduating from Cambridge in 1581 and going to court in 1584, he lived at Lamphey. Robert became so enamoured of the rural life, he later felt that he 'could well have bent his mind to a retired course'.

In 1604, a year after the accession of James I (1603–25), Essex's son of thirteen — Robert, the third earl (d. 1646) — was restored to his family inheritance. Lamphey itself, however, had in the

A portrait of Robert Devereux, second earl of Essex (d. 1601), the flamboyant favourite of the ageing Queen Elizabeth I (1558–1603). Essex spent several years at the family home at Lamphey before going to court in 1584. He died at the block on Tower Hill in February 1601 (Marquess of Tavistock and the Trustees of the Bedford Estate).

meantime been leased to a Carmarthenshire man, Rhys Philip Scarfe. In 1610, supporters of the late earl brought a case before the Star Chamber, claiming that Scarfe had entered the palace at the head of a band of 'disordered and vagrant persons', seized goods worth £400, and corn worth £200, together with 400 sheep. It seems this was a clear move to eject the innocent Scarfe from Lamphey, in an attempt to restore it in full to Robert Devereux.

At the outbreak of the Civil War in 1642, Lamphey was the home of Major John Gunter. He was leasing the estate from Earl Robert, who, though lord chamberlain to King Charles I (1625–49), became commander in chief of the Parliamentary army in 1642. Lamphey Palace was thus garrisoned for Parliament, and Pembroke was provisioned from its stores.

As the first winter of the war closed in, a Captain Crowe raided cattle from the estate to feed Royalist units in Carmarthenshire. Of the buildings in the palace we have no firm record, though it has been suggested they suffered to some degree during the war.

In 1683, the estate was sold to the Owens of Orielton, who did little more than maintain the park and convert the palace to farm buildings. In 1821, Charles Mathias (d. 1851) bought Lamphey and built the nearby Lamphey Court in the neo-classical style, with parts of the palace ruins and the grounds turned into a walled garden. The positioning of the house, and its relationship to the ruins and the medieval church, was very much influenced by Picturesque ideals. In 1925 Mr C. R. Mathias placed the palace in the guardianship of the State. It is now maintained by Cadw: Welsh Historic Monuments.

As a postscript, we might note that the bishop's palace was 'garrisoned' for a second time during the Second World War, when a number of army and RAF units had barracks in the grounds. The concrete bases of their huts can still be found in the trees to the east of the main buildings, and a concrete badge of the Manchester Regiment has survived.

At the outbreak of the Civil War in 1642, Lamphey was already leased by Robert Devereux, third earl of Essex (d. 1646) to Major John Gunter. Earl Robert is shown here in his role as commander in chief of the Parliamentary army. Lamphey was garrisoned for Parliament and supplied provisions for Pembroke — the most prominent Parliamentary base in Wales (Ashmolean Museum, Oxford).

By the end of the eighteenth century, the once handsome medieval palace had been converted to farm buildings. This aquatint shows the site from the south, as seen by Paul Sandby (1730/31–1809), about 1775 (National Library of Wales, P 943).

LAMPHEY PALACE
THE DEVELOPMENT OF THE BUILDINGS

BEFORE THE BLACK BOOK

The earliest surviving building at Lamphey is the ruinous first-floor hall and service rooms once set above an undercroft with a timber ceiling. This block now lies near the centre of the present complex. It is built directly on to a rock outcrop, which suggests that the site may have been surrounded by a dry ditch. None of the finer details of the original door and windows of the building is visible, but the general shape suggests an earlier thirteenth-century date.

Some fifty years later, a much larger and more splendid hall was built against the western end of the initial building. This second hall was also situated at first-floor level, again above an undercroft with a wooden ceiling. The building was constructed with a massive, almost brooding southern façade, and with a buttress at one corner, a stair tower at the other, and a projecting bay at the centre. The hall was entered from a doorway on the north side, and was well lit by four large lancet windows. The handsome carved details in both the windows and the doorway were cut from fine Bath stone. With this new block in place, it seems the older hall was converted into the palace kitchen and associated service rooms. About the same time, a walled courtyard was raised to the north of the new hall.

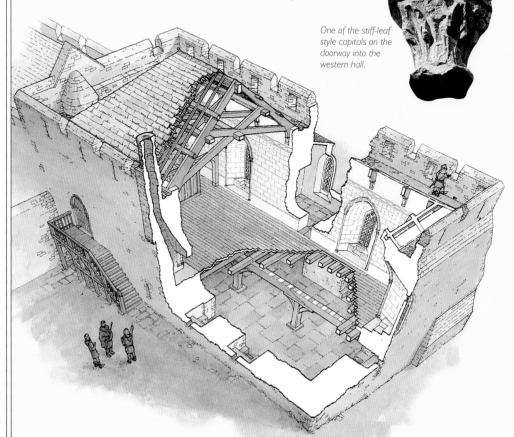

One of the stiff-leaf style capitals on the doorway into the western hall.

A reconstruction of the western hall as it may have appeared when first constructed during the episcopate of Bishop Richard Carew. The floor of the hall was supported on massive oak joists that were carried on an even larger bridging joist along the length of the room (Illustration by Chris Jones-Jenkins, 1991).

AFTER THE BLACK BOOK

The next major phase of construction was probably undertaken during the episcopate of Bishop Henry de Gower, who also built the magnificent palace at St Davids itself. Henry's range is at the eastern end of the site, on lower ground and at an angle to the other buildings. At first it was not linked to the earlier buildings. On the ground floor there is a long vaulted undercroft, initially lit by five small windows. The first floor does not sit neatly on the west wall of the undercroft, which may have survived from an earlier building. This upper floor appears to have been planned as a single undivided great hall, with a small chamber and latrine projecting southwards. It must be said, the quality of detail in this hall is far inferior to that of Bishop Henry's work at St Davids, and this has led several authorities to suggest that the Lamphey building may be later in date. It could have been raised by one of de Gower's successors, mimicking his mason's distinctive style, but failing to achieve quite the same degree of elegance.

Soon after 1500, the western hall block was extensively remodelled, perhaps by Bishop Sherborne, in a style much influenced by the contemporary work of Sir Rhys ap Thomas at nearby Carew Castle. Three-light rectangular windows were inserted into the thirteenth-century openings. To the south, the central window was removed and a small chamber added. The timber ceiling in the undercroft was replaced by a line of masonry vaults, and stone gables were added to support the roof. An upper floor was inserted into the hall itself. The access into de Gower's hall was also altered.

Contemporary with the work may have been the addition of the inner gatehouse, together with the crenellated garden wall and the tiny tower to the south. Though crowned with an arcaded battlement stage, typical of the style associated with de Gower, the gate is far more in keeping with late medieval or even sixteenth-century buildings. The gate may have led from an outer courtyard of storehouses, or perhaps a walled garden, into an inner precinct where the main accommodation can be found.

The last episcopal buildings added to the palace were the work of Bishop Edward Vaughan, sometime before 1522. It was Vaughan who appears to have commissioned the chapel block which was attached to the northern wall of the old hall. Bishop Vaughan also turned his attention to estate matters, and was responsible for the construction of a huge corn barn. The lower courses of its northern wall now form part of the boundary on the north side of the precinct.

LATER WORKS

Despite more than one hundred years in the hands of the Devereux family, Lamphey does not appear to have been modified significantly in the later sixteenth and seventeenth centuries. Two corner fireplaces and a tall chimney are the only clear alterations undertaken.

During the eighteenth century, parts of the ruins were converted to farm buildings. A large cart entrance was created below the chapel window, and there is evidence for a tall lean-to structure — perhaps a small barn — against the northern side of the western hall. Much, however, was no doubt swept away during the nineteenth century when the site was converted into a walled garden. The precinct walls were repaired and a new western boundary constructed. The brick-backed walls of the hot-houses of this period remain.

Although much mutilated, Bishop Henry de Gower's effigy on his tomb lid in the cathedral church at St Davids remains an impressive reminder of his building achievements here and elsewhere in the diocese.

Henry de Gower's hall at Lamphey is distinguished by the arcaded parapet, which is similar, but not identical, to that found at St Davids Bishop's Palace.

The western hall block was remodelled soon after 1500, perhaps by Bishop Robert Sherborne (1505–08). This painting of Sherborne on a wooden panel in the north transept of Chichester Cathedral is thought to date from around 1520.

Although tranquil today, the palace buildings would have been bustling with activity when the medieval bishops and their retinues were in residence at Lamphey. The rising ground beyond the courtyard complex was part of the park that surrounded the palace in the Middle Ages, and provided the basis for a thriving agricultural economy (Skyscan Balloon Photography, for Cadw: Welsh Historic Monuments).

A TOUR OF LAMPHEY PALACE

The palace grounds are entered today via the ticket office and shop, situated in what is the north-west corner of the nineteenth-century walled garden. However, you arrived within the former medieval precinct when driving up the approach road (see plan), crossing the dam of the former fishpond, and passing through the remains of the outer gatehouse.

This tour begins with the main complex of buildings which lie diagonally across the lawns to the far right. As you walk, you will have an opportunity to appreciate the full extent of the palace precinct. Indeed, it extended beyond the modern fence directly ahead of the entrance, well into the rough grazing and trees to the east. It is now a very tranquil and peaceful scene, but would have been bustling with activity when the medieval bishops and their retinues were in residence.

THE WESTERN HALL

On the far side of the now isolated inner gatehouse (pp. 23–4) — with its distinctive arcaded parapet — the first block you approach is the formidable western hall block. There was once a small courtyard or walled garden on this side of the main residential buildings, and parts of the northern wall and the tall eastern wall (through which a later archway has been inserted) still survive.

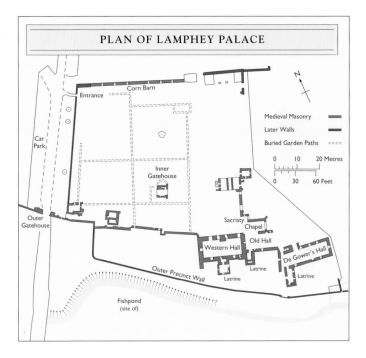

PLAN OF LAMPHEY PALACE

Entrance
Corn Barn
Car Park
Medieval Masonry
Later Walls
Buried Garden Paths
0   10   20 Metres
0   30   60 Feet
Inner Gatehouse
Outer Gatehouse
Sacristy
Chapel
Western Hall
Old Hall
De Gower's Hall
Latrine
Outer Precinct Wall
Latrine
Latrine
Fishpond (site of)

On this northern side of the block, you will see that the main entrance to the hall itself was situated at first-floor level, through the finely carved Bath-stone doorway near the left-hand corner. Remains of a capital with its stiff-leaf decoration survive on the right-hand side of the door arch. The doorway itself must have been reached by a covered wooden staircase, the massive sockets for the supports being visible alongside the sill of the door. Also on this side is the rear of the original chimney, which projects out from the wall face and has Bath-stone quoins. There are unusual carved pendants at the base, and it is topped by a squat, circular stack. One of the thirteenth-century window openings survives at the far right-hand

end, but its details have been robbed away. Finally, it is worth noting that this same western end of the hall was originally intended to be free-standing, though it is now butted by a later precinct wall.

The thirteenth-century entrance to the ground floor of the building is that located directly beneath the hall doorway. The other round-headed openings were created when a line of stone barrel vaults was put into the undercroft about 1500. Inside, there is clear evidence to show that the ceiling of the undercroft was originally a wooden construction. It was carried on massive oak joists set into the sockets along each side. In turn, these were supported on an even larger bridging joist, one socket of which can be seen in the

The courtyard side of the western hall, probably begun by Bishop Richard Carew in the mid-thirteenth century. The entrance to the hall was by way of a first-floor doorway, seen to the left of this view.

A view into the western hall looking towards the west end. The original thirteenth-century hall must have been a very grand room of elegant proportions, and it appears to have been made even more comfortable when it was remodelled around 1500.

eastern end wall, and which ran along the full length of the centre of the room. The bridging joist was itself carried on a line of 'samson posts', forming a wooden arcade (see reconstruction drawing, p. 12). The undercroft was probably lit by five small windows, of which three blocked examples survive set in deep, stepped embrasures. Traces of the later stone barrel vaults can be seen at either end of the undercroft, particularly at the western end. The doorway in the south-east corner led to a spiral staircase which passed between the walls of the two halls, right up to the parapet walkway.

The hall itself occupied virtually the whole of the upper floor, and was open through to its roof. The door in the north-eastern corner opened into a passage, situated behind a wooden screen which kept out the draughts from the hall. Looking up, you will see two small stone cupboards surviving alongside this former passage. The room was lit by tall, two-light windows whose openings were framed by shafts crowned with stiff-leaf capitals. All of the window opening details themselves were lost when they were remodelled around 1500, and much of the stone dressings have been hacked out by later stone robbers.

Between the two windows on the southern side is a section of blank wall, but with a small door leading into a right-angled projection from the hall (not visible). The ground-floor level of this projection is stone vaulted and has a loop opening, though the upper part was lost in a later extension. It was no more than a rather tiny room under a lean-to roof. However, its position implies that the bishop's table was opposite the fireplace, and this projection housed a small antechamber for his use. This was not the normal medieval practice, where the lord's table was at the opposite end to the screens passage. Most of the fireplace itself has collapsed, but it probably had an elaborate stone hood carried on corbels.

The supports of the original roof are difficult to see. They consist of a line of corbels in a dark purple stone (most having been snapped off), with two blocks of Bath stone above. The easiest to find are on the west wall above the window (notice that one corbel is carved as a human head). To begin

with, there were eleven along each side, one in each corner and three across the end walls. They probably carried a 'hipped' roof whose outline was largely hidden by the castellated parapet.

In all, the thirteenth-century western hall was a very grand room of elegant proportions, measuring some 56 feet by 25 feet (17m by 7.5m). It was designed to provide extensive and uninterrupted views to the south, across the fishpond towards the village church, and to the west down the valley of the stream. Some of its magnificence can be appreciated by climbing the spiral staircase up from the undercroft and looking back into the hall from its true floor level.

Around 1500, when it was again to become the centre of the palace complex, the hall underwent a series of fairly major alterations. The large thirteenth-century windows were partly blocked, and rectangular windows with three round-headed lights were inserted. You will see that the example in the south-eastern corner is the most complete. On the outside, the hood moulds of these windows take the form of carved stone angels who hold shields which probably bore the bishop's arms.

At the same time, another floor was rather crudely inserted over the hall, just above the line of the window heads. The stone gables were added and the roof was raised

THE PAINTED DECORATION AT LAMPHEY PALACE

Within the western hall, and in one place in the old hall, you will notice the remains of painted decoration. The walls have two layers of plaster, the top layer being very fine, a rich cream colour, and rubbed to a smooth finish. On this base, a pattern has been painted in red ochre mimicking the joints in ashlar stonework. Single horizontal lines and pairs of vertical lines mark individual blocks of stone. High up in the south-west corner of the western hall are fragments of a border with festoons in red paint set within an inscribed design.

In the window splays, the pattern appears more complicated. There are diagonal rows of five-petalled rosettes, set within the mock-ashlar panels

which have been drawn to give a perspective effect. Much harder to see are the stems of the flowers, painted in yellow ochre, which curve and sweep across the decorated stonework, as if using the ashlar pattern as a trellis. With the whole room painted in this style, there would have been no need for hangings or other decoration.

A similar style of painting has been found in a range of important medieval buildings, including the chapel at nearby Manorbier Castle, which also has other elements added. At Cleeve Abbey in Somerset there are extensive traces of just the same pattern as Lamphey. Elsewhere in Wales, something similar can be seen further east at Chepstow

Castle and Tintern Abbey. The style is by no means uncommon in thirteenth-century buildings, and at Lamphey it is very likely to date from the construction of the western hall.

A detail of the painted plaster in the window splay of the south-eastern window in the western hall. Here you can see a red rosette and the red lines that mimic the joints in ashlar stonework.

to rest on the top of the walls. A new doorway was inserted through the eastern gable and a window put into the western gable. This new second floor must have been divided into chambers, probably lit by dormer windows. Meanwhile, the right-angled projection at the centre of the block had been extended southwards and a chamber and latrine were added.

One of the more interesting survivals in this block as a whole are the traces of painted decoration. They are most easily seen on the plaster at the head of the window in the south-east corner. The cream surface is divided into panels by red lines, and in the centre of some of the panels is a red rosette. Fainter traces of the same decoration can be found elsewhere and it has been partly

restored on the wall of the south-west corner of the hall. This scheme of decoration must have filled the hall, giving it a much brighter and more colourful appearance than today. It can be found in one place in the old hall and may have occurred throughout the living quarters. The only alteration made to this room by the Devereux family was the insertion of the corner fireplace.

A reconstruction of the western hall, as it may have appeared around 1510 (compare with illustration on p. 12), after it was substantially remodelled by Bishop Robert Sherborne (1505–08). By this time, vaulted undercrofts had been inserted, the windows on the first floor modified, and a third stage with dormer windows added to the top of the block (Illustration by Chris Jones-Jenkins, 1991).

THE OLD HALL

Leaving the western hall by the way you came in, and turning immediately around to the right — through what is a large break in its former north wall — you enter the more ruinous block which accommodated the so-called old hall. By the later Middle Ages, this stood at the centre of the main palace complex. It began, however, as a completely free-standing structure measuring some 50 feet by 21 feet (14m by 6.5m), and the remains represent the earliest surviving building on the site.

Once again, the hall and attendant service rooms were situated on the first floor and were set above an undercroft.

Little survives of the ground-floor undercroft, though there was a wooden ceiling carried on a line of corbels, some of which survive. You will see evidence of a blocked doorway into the undercroft on the north side, and at least two blocked slit windows. Even less survives of the hall above. It, too, had a door (now blocked) opening into the northern side, and this was flanked by two lancet windows. There is a similar window on the south side, and on the west wall the line of the steeply pitched roof can be traced.

Since the function of the hall kept changing, all the remainder of the fabric is the result of later alterations. When the western hall was built up against this earlier building, the two blocks were

The site of the old hall, built in the early thirteenth century, is now in a somewhat ruinous state. Originally built as a free-standing structure, it has been much modified through the centuries, traces of which survive in the adjoining walls of the western hall and chapel. The tall chimney is probably an Elizabethan addition to the original southern wall.

Something of the arrangement of the northern wall of the old hall survives in what is now the southern exterior wall of the chapel.

The chapel block was added by Bishop Edward Vaughan (1509–22) sometime before 1522. The fine late Perpendicular east window still survives.

linked by a doorway at first-floor level. A two-storey wing with vaulted roofs and a latrine was added at the south-western corner, and the entire range was probably converted into a kitchen, buttery and pantry for the new western hall.

In turn, when the western hall was remodelled around 1500, this older block was also raised in height. A new fireplace, windows and doors were added to make a suite of rooms. On the north side, a round-headed window was inserted into one of the earlier openings. Originally this had been an outer wall, but the later window must have looked into the chapel. More faint traces of the painted decoration observed in the western hall can be seen at this point. On the opposite side of the block, the tall round chimney is probably an addition of Elizabethan date.

THE CHAPEL

The chapel block was built by Bishop Vaughan in the angle between the old hall and the inner courtyard wall. It may have replaced an earlier building on the same site, or perhaps one located elsewhere in the precinct. The chapel itself was at first-floor level, and its fine late Perpendicular window survives. Notice that the tracery at the head has few cusps, giving the window very clean lines. Part of another window survives on the north side. The small square projection at the north-west corner of the chapel would have contained the sacristy.

Beneath the chapel were two small chambers lit by lines of mullioned windows, but in

the eighteenth century a large archway was inserted beneath the main east chapel window, giving access to what had by then become a farmyard.

HENRY DE GOWER'S HALL

Beyond the old hall and the chapel, on slightly lower ground, you will arrive at the distinctive building known as Henry de Gower's hall. It was added to the eastern end of the earlier sections of the complex, if not by Bishop Henry, then by one of his successors imitating his style of construction. The hall with its undercroft stands below the rock scar, and is placed at an angle to the other ranges. It appears to have been intended as an independent block, set

curiously apart from the remaining rooms at Lamphey. This perhaps implies that it was not a true domestic hall, for it had no service rooms and did not have immediate access to a private chamber. It may have been intended for use on ceremonial occasions, and perhaps acted as the manorial courtroom. Indeed, such distinct ceremonial halls — occurring alongside those for private domestic use — can be found at other episcopal palaces, including St Davids itself, and further afield at Lincoln and at Wells.

The long, cool undercroft here at Lamphey runs the full length of the ground floor. The original entrance is underneath the flight of external steps. Inside, the barrel vault was carried on eleven arched stone ribs, of which only the stumps remain. There were six narrow

The interior of Henry de Gower's hall, looking east. The room may have been used on ceremonial occasions, and perhaps acted as the manorial courtroom. The round chimney in the far corner was an addition made during the Devereux ownership of the palace in the Elizabethan period.

The long, vaulted undercroft runs the full length of the ground floor beneath Henry de Gower's hall. This cool room was used for storage and perhaps served as the bishop's wine cellar, though the addition of a fireplace and cross passage suggests that it was later occupied by palace servants.

windows with trefoiled heads along the sides (some now altered or blocked) and one in the eastern end. This room was for storage, and perhaps served as the palace's wine cellar. As elsewhere at Lamphey, there were later modifications to this basement chamber, with a passage created across its western end and a small fireplace constructed within the width of the south wall, possibly when the undercroft became living quarters for palace servants. Near the fireplace there is a somewhat unexpected graffito: 'THIS IS NOT DRINKING WATER'. In fact, it dates from the army's occupation of the ruins during the last war.

On leaving the undercroft, you should climb the flight of steps into de Gower's hall itself. The steps were initially covered by a roof carried on wooden posts and on the two corbels projecting from the wall. It was a common practice in medieval great houses and abbeys to link buildings by covered walks or lean-to roofs, keeping occupants dry in wet weather and shaded in high summer.

The hall remains an impressive single room, with no evidence for the usual 'screens passage' and service rooms at the entrance end. With overall measurements of about 70 feet by 18 feet (21m by 5.5m), it is a notably long and yet rather narrow

chamber. It was lit by six two-light windows — rather irregularly spaced — each with stone seats in the embrasure. There is no evidence that any of these windows were ever glazed, though the traces of rebated edges suggest they were probably fitted with wooden shutters. Near the centre of the southern wall, there is a small fireplace, whose tiny chimney alongside also serves the later fireplace in the undercroft. It seems unlikely that such a small fireplace could have provided heat for so large a space, and there may have been one or two open hearths at the centre of the hall. Indeed, there must have been a similar arrangement in de Gower's main hall at St Davids.

The hall roof was carried on six wooden trusses, sprung from a line of wedge-shaped corbels set about 5 feet (1.5m) above the floor. The line of the original pitched roof is clear at either end, and some of the slates can be seen embedded in the sides of the arcade. This type of arcaded and battlemented parapet occurs at two other sites: the bishop's palace at St Davids and at Swansea Castle — where it is traditionally associated with Bishop Henry de Gower. However, the quality of the workmanship above the Lamphey hall is much the plainest, being constructed of rubble stone, with round and not pointed arches, and lacking the sculpture and chequer-work which is so distinctive at St Davids. At all three sites, however, the parapet served the same functions, that is to throw the rainwater cleanly off the roof and clear of the wall face, and to provide elevated walkways. Here at Lamphey the walkway would have provided fine views of the palace and grounds, and these can still be appreciated by visitors who wish to climb the (narrow and somewhat difficult) spiral staircase to the parapet in the south-west corner.

Near the same corner as the stair, there is another door which gives access to a room set at right angles to the hall. The fact that 'straight joints' exist between the walls of this room and the main block suggest it is a later addition, but it has a window moulded in the same style and in the same stone as those in the hall. The room contains a latrine.

Once again, several alterations were made to de Gower's hall during later periods. The line of the roof was raised at the eastern end, and a latrine and two fireplaces were inserted. The fireplace in the north-east corner still has its Elizabethan round chimney. A passage was created running diagonally from the north-west corner to the remodelled old hall. Before this was built, food must have been carried across the open courtyard and up the flight of steps.

This isolated and somewhat austere looking hall probably fell largely out of use in the fifteenth and sixteenth centuries. Unlike the western hall, there is no evidence of new windows inserted during the later Middle Ages. In 1536, the inventory made for Bishop Rawlins records the only contents as being three pieces of old carpet.

THE 'RED CHAMBER' AND THE INNER GATEHOUSE

Leaving de Gower's hall, and returning past the chapel towards the courtyard area, over to the right you will see a building apparently carried on three arches. When constructed, it was raised against the inner courtyard wall. The upper storey can still be reached by way of an external flight of steps. In the nineteenth century, when Richard Fenton visited Lamphey, it was known as the 'Red Chamber' and it had only recently lost its roof. The room

Although the inner gatehouse now stands in isolation, it was once linked to walls either side of it that separated the inner and outer courtyards.

has a latrine in one corner and was clearly intended for domestic use.

From the doorway of the 'Red Chamber' you will have a good view towards the inner gatehouse. Although it now appears to stand in isolation, stubs of masonry show that it had curtain walls running off to either side. That which ran to the left linked the gate to the small battlemented corner tower which remains standing to the south. As built, the gatehouse and its adjoining walls would have served to separate the bishop's apartments at the heart of the palace complex from the more workaday buildings situated around the outer courtyard.

The top of the gate is crowned with a distinctive arcaded parapet, though it is of a different form from that over de Gower's hall. In particular, the stone here is dressed and the arches are pointed. In general terms this type of non-defensive gatehouse is quite widespread in Wales, often dating from the sixteenth century. But the use of the arcaded parapet could imply an earlier date.

Within the cobbled gate-passage there is a door into an intermural stairway, which leads to the small room above. From here there are further good views of the precinct layout. It appears that the original access to the upper floor of the gatehouse was by way of the now blocked doorway which can be seen in the exterior of the north wall.

The distinctive pink mortar used in the stonework to block various openings in the buildings may represent hasty measures to improve the palace defences at the outbreak of the Civil War in 1642.

THE SOUTHERN PADDOCK AREA

Leaving the gatehouse, you will find a small doorway through the once battlemented wall to the south. This opens into another walled paddock and leads to the exterior of the western hall and de Gower's hall. Indeed, the true scale and splendour of these structures is best appreciated from this southern side.

The outer wall of the paddock has been partly rebuilt, and some of the battlements blocked using a distinctive pink mortar. The same mortar was used in the blocking of the undercroft windows and doors in both de Gower's hall and the western hall. It may represent hasty measures to improve the defences of the palace at the outbreak of the Civil War in the 1640s.

A stream flows across the precinct and runs into a small rectangular pond in the eastern corner of this outer paddock. However, the stream may originally have been diverted

under de Gower's hall and then through a number of ground-level arches to flush out the latrines of the western hall.

THE OUTER COURTYARD

You should return towards the ticket office via the outer courtyard area. Fragments of some of the medieval buildings survive, including what is a sunken cellar in the south-western corner. As a whole, the complex of structures may have included, for example, the oxhouse, the dovecot, and bakehouse or brewhouse, all of which were mentioned in the *Black Book* of 1326.

Turning to the northern precinct wall, to the far left and right you will see the brick rear walls of demolished hot-houses from the last century. But this same wall also contains the remains of one of the largest buildings ever raised by the bishops of St Davids at Lamphey. This was Bishop Edward Vaughan's immense garner or corn barn. A stretch of the lower part of its massive stone walls extends for 130 feet (40m) between the two areas of brickwork and includes six symmetrically placed ventilation slots. The building was designed to store grain from the whole of the Lamphey estate. In the inventory for Bishop Rawlins taken in March 1536 — at the end of the winter — the garner still contained 10 bushels of wheat, 112 bushels of barley malt, and 100 bushels of oats. Even though it is only a fragment of this major building which survives, it is a reminder that the medieval manor at Lamphey was just as important for its agricultural produce as it was as a place for retreat and entertainment for the bishops of St Davids.

The western wall of the precinct, with its small blocked battlements, is entirely a nineteenth-century construction, and you will see other remains of what became the Victorian walled garden. Immediately on the northern side of the inner gatehouse there is a semicircular earthwork, where a fountain once stood. During particularly dry spells, it is also possible to pick out the pattern of hidden garden

pathways showing as parchmarks in the grass.

Finally, as you leave the palace, notice the square nesting boxes in the walls of the medieval outer gatehouse, showing it was later converted into a pigeon house.

All that survives of the great barn are the lower courses of its outer wall — including traces of six ventilation slots — which now form part of the boundary on the north side of the outer courtyard.

A reconstruction of the bishop's palace from the south-east showing how it may have appeared in the early sixteenth century. The outer courtyard, to the top left of this illustration, is dominated by Bishop Vaughan's immense garner or corn barn (Illustration by Chris Jones-Jenkins, 1991).

A BIRD'S-EYE VIEW OF LAMPHEY PALACE
FROM THE WEST

1 Outer gatehouse — *now ruinous, this gave access to the whole of the walled palace precinct. It was later converted into a pigeon house (p. 15, 25).*

2 Fishponds — *although now silted-up and overgrown, the fishponds were an important source of food for the bishop and his retinue (p. 8, 15).*

3 Western hall — *built in the thirteenth century and completely remodelled in the early sixteenth century, this was the most impressive building in the palace. There are remains of thirteenth-century wall paintings (pp. 15–18).*

4 Old hall — *this is the oldest of the palace buildings. It began as a first-floor hall but was later converted to a kitchen and service rooms. The tall chimney is Elizabethan (pp. 19–21).*

5 Chapel — *added by Bishop Vaughan in the early sixteenth century. Its elegant Perpendicular east window survives intact (p. 21).*

6 Henry de Gower's hall — *with its distinctive arcaded parapet was raised above a vaulted undercroft. The hall is almost detached from the other buildings, suggesting that it had a ceremonial rather than a domestic function (pp. 21–3).*

7 'Red Chamber' — *provided additional domestic accommodation (pp. 23–4).*

8 Inner courtyard — *a walled garden or courtyard alongside the entrance to the western hall (pp. 23–4).*

9 Inner gatehouse — *crowned with a finely detailed arcaded parapet, it gave access into the bishop's private apartments away from the bustle of the precinct (pp. 23–4).*

10 Southern paddock — *this area was enclosed perhaps as late as the Civil War period. The scale and magnificence of the palace halls are best appreciated from here (p. 24).*

11 Outer courtyard — *this contains the remains of the storehouses and other buildings necessary for the day-to-day running of the palace (pp. 24–5).*

12 Corn barn — *part of the rear wall of Bishop Vaughan's great garner, built to store the vast quantity of grain from the manor of Lamphey (pp. 24–5).*

(Illustration by John Banbury)

Llawhaden Castle still dominates the skyline above the steep-sided valley of the Eastern Cleddau, with St Aidan's parish church nestling in the foreground below. This imposing site first attracted the Normans to build a castle here, early in the twelfth century. By the eighteenth century, however, this dramatic location had become popular with artists and the castle ruins featured in numerous paintings (see p. 31).

A HISTORY OF LLAWHADEN CASTLE

EARLY HISTORY

Even before the arrival of the Norman invaders, Llawhaden and its ancient church had long formed part of the estates of the bishops of St Davids. But following the death of Wilfred in 1115, it was probably Bishop Bernard — the first of the Norman incumbents — who erected the earliest castle on the site. The earth-and-timber stronghold was one of a line of castles within a shifting frontier known as the *Landsker*. Norman and Flemish settlers lay to the south and west, with the region to the north and east still ruled by Welsh princely chieftains.

Llawhaden Castle was mentioned in passing in 1175, when Gerald of Wales visited his uncle, Bishop David fitz Gerald (1148–76), at the site. Then, less than two decades later, in 1192 the castle was captured by Gerald's cousin, the Lord Rhys (d. 1197). In the Welsh *Chronicle of the Princes* (*Brut y Tywysogyon*) it is recorded that in 1193 'the Welsh gathered together, and they razed the said castle to ground at their pleasure'. Thereafter, Norman control of the area was not fully recovered until the early years of the thirteenth century. It was probably at this time that the castle was refortified with a stone curtain wall and a number of circular towers.

BISHOP THOMAS BEK (1280–93)

An account of 1280 records the expenses paid to a janitor at Llawhaden Castle. In June of that same year, Thomas Bek became bishop of St Davids, and he was to take a great interest in developing the manor of Llawhaden. Born into a Lincolnshire baronial family, Bek entered clerical orders to follow a career in government and politics. Clearly an able man and a good administrator, he became chancellor of the university of Oxford in 1269, and from 1274 until 1280 he was keeper of the wardrobe to King Edward I (1272–1307) — one of the two most important government posts of the day. During this period, Bek was rewarded with a number of ecclesiastical benefices or incomes, greatly increasing his personal wealth. His appointment to the bishopric of St Davids came in June 1280. He was in fact one of eight royal wardrobe clerks rewarded with an episcopal mitre by Edward I.

Bishop Bek set out energetically to develop the see of St Davids. He reorganized the cathedral chapter and was responsible for various modifications to the layout of the cathedral close. He founded colleges of priests at Llangadog (later moved to Abergwili) and Llanddewi Brefi, and he established three new boroughs within the diocesan estates, at St Davids, New Moat and Llawhaden. These new boroughs were market towns in which the burgesses (freemen of the borough) were freed from their feudal duties, allowing them to develop trade and new industries, with the bishop as landlord collecting the rents and tolls.

Llawhaden was Bek's most ambitious foundation. In 1281, he was granted royal licence to hold a weekly market and two annual three-day fairs, which together provided the basis of the borough's economy. Six years later, he founded a hospital for the poor and aged on the western edge of the growing

The seal of Bishop Thomas Bek (1280–93), who, although much concerned with the borough of Llawhaden, appears to have taken little interest in the castle buildings themselves (Society of Antiquaries).

borough. By 1326, some 174 tenement plots, each of about 4½ acres (1.8ha), had been let to 126 burgesses, the large majority of whom were Englishmen. In all, the rental of these plots, the market dues and tolls, and the leasing of the watermill, fulling mill, and fishery in the river, made Llawhaden the richest estate held by the bishops of St Davids. And yet despite all this interest in the manor, there is no hard evidence that Bishop Bek invested any resources in the rebuilding of the castle or its accommodation.

BISHOP ADAM DE HOUGHTON (1362–89)

In a survey of the bishop's estates taken in 1327, Llawhaden is described as having a castle worth nothing beyond the outlay. In 1342, Bishop Henry de Gower issued an order to keep only seven of his residences in repair, one of which was the castle at Llawhaden. It appears, however, that it was not until the episcopate of Adam de Houghton that the early thirteenth-century structure was radically redeveloped. Bishop Adam had been the precentor or dean of St Davids from 1339 until 1350, and he was to be the royal chancellor under Edward III (1327–77) in the last year of the king's reign. In 1365, with John of Gaunt, duke of Lancaster (d. 1399), and Blanche the duke's wife (d. 1369), the bishop founded St Mary's College alongside the cathedral church, though the building was not completed until 1384.

As a friend of Lancaster, and later a privy counsellor to King Richard II (1377–99), de Houghton moved in court circles. He chose to accept fashionable Perpendicular designs for St Mary's College and Llawhaden Castle. His master mason was John Fawle or Fawley, who in 1383 was described as 'master of our works',

The seal of Bishop Adam de Houghton, who initiated an extensive campaign of building work, which transformed Llawhaden Castle in the later years of the fourteenth century (Public Record Office, DL 27/102).

and who was appointed by the bishop to the constableship of Llawhaden. In the same year Fawle was given licence to collect rushes for the chambers in the castle complex, implying that the hall and south range apartments (including the chapel) were all complete by this time. The gatehouse may be marginally later in date, raised by Fawle for his own use as constable.

THE LATER MIDDLE AGES

The diocesan registers record a number of edicts issued at Llawhaden at the end of the fourteenth century, showing that the bishops continued to use it as a residence at this time. And in 1403 King Henry IV (1399–1413) ordered the garrisoning of the castle in fear of the Owain Glyn Dŵr rebellion. But for much of the remainder of the fifteenth century the bishops of St Davids appear to have abandoned Llawhaden and the castle was let to commoners.

Bishop Hugh Pavy (1485–96), however, was one to favour the site, and in 1486 he celebrated mass with his diocesan officials in the castle chapel. Two years later he was again at Llawhaden, officiating at the trial of William ap Hugyn, a parish clerk, who was accused of 'ravishing and violating Gwenllian, daughter of David de Trefwalter, and carrying away her goods and chattels'. The wretched William pleaded innocence, and eventually got away with only having to pay expenses to the keeper of the castle dungeon.

Llawhaden's role as the bishop's prison is again emphasized by an episode of 1503. In that year, Thomas Wyriott stormed the castle with a troop of horsemen to free a woman named Tanglwys, who was incarcerated within the walls.

The castle was repaired by Bishop Edward Vaughan (1509–22), but this renewed episcopal interest was short-lived, and on the death of Bishop Rawlins in 1536, the only contents recorded within the building were a feather bed and a few small items worth just 13s. 4d. The next bishop, the somewhat infamous William Barlow (1536–48), stripped the lead from the roofs of the castle as part of his scheme to move the centre of power in the diocese to Carmarthen. From this time onwards, Llawhaden began to fall into decay. The process

By the later Middle Ages, Llawhaden served as the bishop's prison: there is a deep dungeon in the base of the chapel tower. This pair of handcuffs was discovered at Llawhaden (National Museum of Wales).

was almost completed wholesale when Bishop Richard Milbourne (1615–21) was given licence to demolish the castle in 1616. The site may have been saved from complete ruin by his transfer to the diocese of Carlisle.

LATER HISTORY

The imposing position of Llawhaden Castle, high above the road from Carmarthen to Haverfordwest, attracted many visitors and artists in more recent centuries, and their works record the steady decline of the building.

The view of 1740 by the Buck brothers shows the parapets in place above the gatehouse and towers, and windows surviving in a wing of the hall range. Richard Fenton, writing of a visit made in 1810, bemoaned that 'this venerable ruin has been plundered most shamefully and unnecessarily to supply materials for repairing the roads ... and it is to be lamented that the bishops of St. David's are not induced to prohibit such depredations on that majestic structure'.

Eventually they were to do so, for in the last quarter of the nineteenth century the Ancient Monuments Committee for Pembrokeshire undertook the care and conservation of the ruins of Llawhaden. In 1931 the castle was placed in the guardianship of the ancient monuments branch of the Office of Works.

One unexpected but glorious legacy of this period of decay is the wealth of wild flowers which remain in the moat of the castle. Over one hundred plant species have been identified, representing a range of the flowers which must have been found in the meadows and woodlands of Pembrokeshire before modern methods of agriculture so altered the local environment.

This distant view of Llawhaden Castle and St Aidan's church, painted by John 'Warwick' Smith (1749–1831), typifies eighteenth-century artistic interest in the borough (National Library of Wales, PD 9343).

LLAWHADEN CASTLE
THE DEVELOPMENT OF THE BUILDINGS

A reconstruction of the castle as it may have appeared towards the end of the Middle Ages. The hall block to the rear and the southern range in the foreground were all part of the major programme of construction undertaken by Bishop Adam de Houghton (1362–89) in the late fourteenth century (Illustration by Chris Jones-Jenkins, 1991).

THE TWELFTH AND THIRTEENTH CENTURIES

The remains of Llawhaden Castle show several distinct phases of construction, and the appearance of the buildings is likely to have changed considerably during the Middle Ages. The earliest castle was probably raised as a 'ringwork', comprising the present dry ditch which in turn encircled a stone-and-earth rampart made of dug out material. This ringwork may well have been adapted from an earlier Iron Age banked-and-ditched enclosure, a great number of which survive in this area. Either way, the inner bank would have stood to a substantial height and is likely to have been crowned by a wooden palisade and walkway. A wooden

gateway no doubt provided access to the interior of the castle, where there is likely to have been a range of timber buildings, including a hall, stables, kitchen and outhouses.

Llawhaden was captured in 1192 by the Lord Rhys and was destroyed in 1193 (p. 29). The English bishops of St Davids did not recapture the site until early in the thirteenth century. It was after this that stone defences were constructed, based on a circular tower, the footings of which survive and show it to have been some 28 feet (8.5m) in diameter. This tower was connected to a curtain wall built of many short, straight stretches, with the additional defence of at least one other smaller circular tower. The square tower immediately behind the eastern half of the late medieval

gatehouse — containing four latrine shafts — is probably of this same period. Stone buildings may also have appeared in the interior of the castle.

THE FOURTEENTH CENTURY AND LATER WORKS

The survey of Llawhaden undertaken in 1326 refers to 'the stone buildings within the walls' and 'the wooden buildings outside the walls'. Two gardens were also mentioned; one of an acre (0.4ha), the small field due east of the castle, and another — 'the park' — of four acres (1.6ha) lying to the north-east. But another survey taken in the following year described Llawhaden as a stone castle worth nothing per annum beyond the outlay, suggesting that there may have been little or no new building for almost a century.

A major new programme of construction began in the third quarter of the fourteenth century, initiated by Bishop Adam de Houghton (1362–89) and designed by John Fawle. Through a grant of 1383, Fawle was appointed constable of the castle and was described by the bishop as 'master of our works'. At the same time, Fawle was completing work on the bishop's college of St Mary — the chapel and cloister of which stand alongside the cathedral at St Davids (pp. 4–5).

The work began with the rectangular hall block facing the gateway to the castle, and progressed towards the south range with its first-floor chapel. The builders retained fragments of the thirteenth-century curtain wall within the outer walls of the new south range. On the courtyard side, it was to be entered independently by way of a tall, narrow porch. The chapel tower lay at the eastern end of the range and was connected via the curtain wall to the bishop's private chamber in the hall block. The remainder of the south range housed suites of apartments or lodgings for the bishop's retinue or guests. These lodgings may have

extended over to the other side of the gatehouse where the ruins of another vaulted basement survive. All of this work may have been completed by 1383. The gatehouse seems to have been added a little later. It is similar in form to the gatehouse at Carmarthen Castle, built about 1410 in the aftermath of the Glyn Dŵr rebellion. Indeed, Henry IV (1399–1413) had ordered the garrisoning of Llawhaden during the uprising.

These new towers and the gatehouse together give the castle a formidable external appearance, especially when viewed from the south. But the work was intended more as a display of episcopal status than for any form of serious defence. The interior façades certainly betray a well-appointed and fashionable residence. In the later fourteenth century, members of the court circle were fascinated by the concept of chivalry and knightly display, whilst at the same time they also had to provide accommodation in keeping with a more elaborate social life and growing numbers of retainers. The conversion of earlier castles into residences of this new type was begun by King Edward III (1327–77) at Windsor, and was developed by John of Gaunt (d. 1399) at Kenilworth in Warwickshire, and by Richard II (1377–99) at Portchester

in Hampshire. The combination of a projecting closet tower serving pairs of apartments can be found at Amberley Castle in Sussex, a residence rebuilt by the bishops of Chichester from about 1377. A tall, narrow tower similar to the five-storey porch at Llawhaden can be found on top of the late fourteenth-century keep at Warkworth Castle in Northumberland. And long ranges of lodgings — usually divided into small cells — became commonplace from the last quarter of the fourteenth century. Examples include the cellular lodgings of Dartington Hall in Devon, begun about 1389 by Richard II's half-brother, John de Holand (d. 1400). The reconstruction of Llawhaden Castle was very much part of this tradition and demonstrates the sophistication of both the bishop and the mason responsible.

It is difficult to identify any later phases of building activity in the surviving fabric at Llawhaden with any real clarity. None the less, in 1541 the antiquary John Leland recorded that Bishop Vaughan (1509–22) had rebuilt the chapel and undertaken general repairs at the site. This cannot be confirmed today. Certainly after the Reformation, the castle rapidly fell into decay.

This 1734 engraving of Dartingon Hall, Devon, by Samuel and Nathaniel Buck, shows the cellular lodgings. A similar arrangement was built for the comfort of the bishop's guests in the south range at Llawhaden (Society of Antiquaries).

An aerial view of the castle showing the gatehouse and southern range in the foreground. The design and construction of much of what is visible today appears to have been in the hands of John Fawle, master of the bishop's works (Skyscan Balloon Photography, for Cadw: Welsh Historic Monuments).

A TOUR OF LLAWHADEN CASTLE

THE GATEHOUSE

The castle is entered through its tall, twin-towered gatehouse which — due to the collapse of much of the rear masonry — now rises almost like a stage set. The two D-shaped towers emerge from deeply spurred bases and they are joined above the gate-passage by a segmental arch. The upper half of the gate as a whole is decorated with a bold display of decorated bands in purple Caerbwdy stone, quarried near St Davids. The trefoil-headed windows in the higher level are quite large, featuring both mullions and transoms. Above the central window there was clearly a projecting gallery or system of 'machicolation'. Three arched openings, supported on central lion's head corbels and springers to either side, served as 'murder holes' through which missiles could be dropped on attackers at the gate below. The arrowslits around the two lower stages of the gatehouse gave a range of fire out across the moat and drawbridge.

The stone-walled enclosure outside the gatehouse to the left is of relatively recent date. It served as the village pinfold, or pound for stray animals.

When first completed, the gatehouse was approached across a wooden drawbridge. One of its pivot stones survives in situ, low down within the right-hand side of the entrance.

Directly above are the remains of the slot for the portcullis. To either side of the entrance passage are vaulted cellars, and — as the slope rises — you pass through the line of the earlier curtain wall. Turning around, and looking up, you will see that the gatehouse contained a number of spacious and well-lit stone-vaulted rooms, many with their own fireplace and comfortable window seats. Together, these rooms provided accommodation for the constable and his family. He was the man who ran the castle and its associated borough during the bishop's absence.

The front of the castle gatehouse. The large windows, stone carving and bands of purple Caerbwdy stone suggest an emphasis on decorative rather than defensive qualities, despite the presence of murder holes and low-level arrowslits.

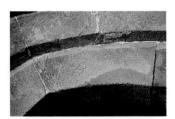

A mason's mark — which served to identify a mason's work — cut in one of the stones of the arch above the doorway into the hall undercroft.

THE HALL

Directly across the courtyard from the gatehouse are the remains of the massive, though sadly ruined, great hall. Essentially, it was a free-standing block, with the hall situated on the first floor above an undercroft or storehouse. Cross-wings flanked either end of the central range, each one projecting out over the edge of the ditch.

On the courtyard side, the large triple-chamfered door arch at the centre of the range led into the main undercroft. To the right of the doorway there is a cusped, single-light window — one of three which once gave a little light to the vast undercroft. Note that for some reason the big bulbous stops to either side of the base of the door are finished at different heights, and on some of the arch stones above you will find a distinct Z-shaped mason's mark. In the rebates just behind the arch are the remains of the great iron hinges which carried the door,

The once massive great hall block lies directly across the courtyard from the gatehouse. The hall was situated on the first floor above a vast vaulted undercroft. Cross wings at either end of the hall provided service rooms and private accommodation for the bishop.

A view along the length of the hall from the service end, looking towards the bishop's private chamber or solar in the cross wing at the far end of the building.

together with the slots which took the wooden drawbar used to keep it barred.

Inside, the undercroft was a single long room, though much of the outer wall and barrel vault have collapsed. From here there is a fine view up the valley of the Eastern Cleddau towards the Preseli mountains. The doorway in what is the western corner leads to a flight of spiral steps (now blocked) which gave access to the hall above. At the other end of the

undercroft, there are two small cupboards cut within the wall. The hall itself, measuring some 79 feet long by 23 feet wide (24m by 7m), was placed directly over this undercroft.

You should now retrace your steps back outside and look up. The doorway into the hall was above and to the left of the undercroft door. To begin with, it was probably approached by stone steps rising from the left and ending above the projecting masonry pier. However, the construction of the bakehouse (p. 41) would have cut off the base of these stairs, and the line of steps seems to have been turned over to the other side of the door. The position of the replacement steps can be traced by the surviving pattern of plaster on the walls. Their line passed across the undercroft window and then on to the right-hand masonry pier. The evidence for a roof crease suggests there was a timber structure overhead, carried to the front on posts. Above the undercroft doorway, there may have been a porch

of two storeys, with the first floor supported by the projecting stone corbels. The most intriguing feature is the slot running up the face of the wall. It may have served to house one side of a door which could be dropped to block the top of the stair, or it may have been the position where the timber wall of the porch was secured to the main block.

At either end of the central hall block, the cross-wings each had their own independent stone-vaulted undercroft. The one to the left may have been the kitchen, linked through service rooms — the buttery, pantry and servery — to the hall itself. A spiral staircase connected the two storeys.

In the cross-wing to the right, the upper floor served as the bishop's private chamber or solar. This large and well-lit room had a broad window overlooking the castle gardens and out into open country. The window is flanked by two small antechambers with latrines, set within the thickness of the walls.

A BIRD'S-EYE VIEW OF LLAWHADEN CASTLE
FROM THE SOUTH-WEST

1 Gatehouse — *added to the castle at the beginning of the fifteenth century. The upper storey provided well-appointed accommodation for the constable and his family (p. 35).*

2 Pound — *an enclosure built over the castle ditch to house stray animals found in the parish, probably in the eighteenth century (p. 35).*

3 Hall block — *a large hall with associated chamber and kitchen, raised over stone-vaulted undercrofts. Large windows on the eastern side of the building gave splendid views over the valley of the Eastern Cleddau (pp. 35–6).*

4 Chapel — *three windows of purple Caerbwdy stone indicate the position of the castle's chapel (p. 38).*

5 Chapel tower — *the ground floor contains a deep dungeon with elegant rooms on the two floors above, each providing fine views (p. 38).*

6 Porch — *the remarkable five-storey porch to the south range rises high above the parapet walls and gave impressive views across the surrounding countryside (p. 40).*

7 Closet tower — *this served the range of four apartments built in the later fourteenth century (p. 40).*

8 Round tower — *the base survives from the first phase of the stone defences of the castle, dating from the early thirteenth century (p. 41).*

9 Bakehouse — *footings of the late medieval bakehouse, added to the kitchen end of the hall (p. 41).*

10 Moat — *a rock-cut and partly water-filled ditch, which was the first line of defence during the whole of the castle's history (p. 42).*

(Illustration by John Banbury)

The chapel on the first floor of the south range can be identified by the line of three windows carved from purple Caerbwdy stone.

THE SOUTH RANGE

The angled south range is formed by a single great suite of rooms. The three undercrofts — the stubs of whose barrel vaults survive — were built against the line of the early thirteenth-century curtain wall. But the rooms above basement level, together with the tall porch and the closet and chapel towers projecting out of the curtain wall, all belong to Bishop Adam de Houghton's reconstruction of the castle in the later fourteenth century.

This major phase of new work also involved the building of the chapel at the eastern end. This is most easily distinguished by the line of three windows whose dressings are made of distinctive purple Caerbwdy stone. Notice that each window had an inner arch cut from the same stone. The recess in the wall above suggests that the chapel had a T-shaped or cruciform roof. The chapel was lined with plaster and was probably richly painted.

The chapel tower was built against the earlier masonry and partly over the castle ditch. The ground floor is reached down a flight of stone steps. It is lit by two rectangular slit windows set high up in deep embrasures. In the centre of the floor is a hole covered by a grille. This is the only access to a deep dungeon cut down into the bedrock, which probably acted as the bishop's prison. Set within the wall of this tower is a passage leading to a tiny latrine.

To reach the rooms in the tower above, you should climb the modern metal staircase. At first-floor level, the octagonal room with the domed roof seems to have had access from the rear of the chapel and may have acted as a vestry, or perhaps the chaplain's chamber. Traces of wall plaster survive, and there is a fireplace and a latrine.

Climbing to the top floor, you will find an even more elegant chamber. This could only be reached by a stairway and passage within the walls and was independent of the chapel. The passage may have led across a short length of curtain wall to the bishop's chamber in the hall block. The room itself has a handsome octagonal groined vault, and perhaps served as the bishop's treasury, or was possibly used for storing court records. From this upper storey, the staircase continued up to the parapet above the tower, and to the wall-walk around the remainder of the south range.

Back at ground level, it is clear to see that the tall porch on the courtyard façade of the chapel was intended to give a grandiose effect to the entire range (see reconstruction drawing p. 40). The porch was entered through what was initially an arched doorway with deeply moulded jambs and a rectangular projecting hood. The label stops at the base of the hood take the form of carved heads, perhaps representing Bishop Adam de Houghton's patrons, John of Gaunt and his wife Blanche.

Right: *The doorway into the south range porch. The label stops at the base of the hood take the form of carved heads and may represent Bishop Adam de Houghton's patrons, John of Gaunt (d. 1399) and his wife, Blanche (d. 1369).*

Below: *A view across the courtyard from the late medieval bakehouse towards the fourteenth-century south range. The tall porch is a distinct and quite unusual feature.*

A reconstruction of the courtyard at Llawhaden as it may have appeared at the beginning of the fifteenth century. To the left, the steps and wooden porch lead up to the hall. To the right is the south range containing comfortable lodgings and the castle chapel (Illustration by Chris Jones-Jenkins, 1991).

Inside, the curving staircase led up to the chapel doorway with its pointed head. At this level, the porch was covered by a quadripartite vault carried on plain shafts in each corner. The staircase continued, in a rather awkward fashion, to a door on the eastern side, giving access to an internal spiral staircase. This opened on to small square rooms, one on each of the next three storeys. The room at the top had windows in each wall and an octagonal vaulted roof. The stairs climb even higher, to the roof level itself, which may have been topped by a small spirelet.

The porch as a whole rises high above the roof tops and over the curtain wall. It was surely designed to provide a lookout over the whole of the Llawhaden estate. There are similarities with Bishop Adam's bell tower at St Mary's chapel in St Davids, and further afield with the tall central tower built on top of the contemporary keep at Warkworth Castle in Northumberland. The porch as a viewing platform does seem to indicate a particularly early appreciation of the beauty of surrounding landscape. Indeed, there is further evidence for the appreciation of natural beauty at this time in the poetry of Dafydd ap Gwilym.

As completed, the northern façade of the range, including the porch, was linked together with a projecting string course, probably interspersed with gargoyles at roof level. Just to the left of the porch, below the level of the string course, there is a small fragment of one of the courtyard windows of the chapel.

To the right of the porch, you will see that the apartments were divided into two sections, each one built over an undercroft. There were four upper chambers in all, one to each storey in both of the sections. The rooms all had a fireplace, and the main windows faced the courtyard. There are two small windows high in the curtain wall, set in deep embrasures with stone window seats. Access to all these rooms must have been from a spiral staircase, the base of which survives in the centre of the northern wall.

The apartments were served by the intervening tower which is built out over the ditch. Internally, this tower is divided down the middle by a spine wall, and on each side of this — at both levels — there are identical vaulted rooms lit by cross-loops. A passage leads from each room to a latrine, whose shaft runs down the middle of the spine wall. These rooms were probably closets or small bed chambers.

All in all, the apartments and the associated rooms within the new gatehouse demonstrate the very full provision of accommodation for the bishop's retinue at Llawhaden. Those staying at the castle would have included other members of the cathedral chapter, the bishop's steward and constable, and various distinguished guests. The extraordinary number of latrines shows the increasing concern for privacy and hygiene, whereas the fireplaces provided a level of comfort not found in the vast halls of earlier medieval episcopal palaces.

THE WEST RANGE

The remainder of the buildings around the courtyard are much more ruinous and more difficult to understand, but they do reveal something of the early history of the site. At the centre of the courtyard is the castle well which reaches a depth of over 100 feet (30m). On the right-hand side of the rear of the gatehouse is yet another building with a vaulted basement. This has two windows opening on to the courtyard, and it has been suggested that this room and those above provided accommodation for the bishop's private garrison. It is set behind the remains of the

early curtain wall and up against the base of a circular tower. This tower must belong to the refortification of the castle early in the thirteenth century, after its destruction by the Lord Rhys in 1193. The tower was perhaps left standing, at least one storey high, for much of the castle's history.

Projecting from the north-western end of the hall range are the footings of a later bakehouse, and the base of one of the ovens can be seen. In the far corner is a stretch of curtain wall, just four courses high. This butts against the hall and overlies the footings of a small circular tower, bringing three phases of the castle's construction together at one point.

The footings of the later medieval bakehouse can be seen built out from the earlier hall block, with the base of one of the ovens in the foreground.

THE EXTERIOR OF THE CASTLE

You may like to complete your tour by looking at part of the outside of the castle, beginning by crossing the ditch between the hall and the south range.

Looking back towards the hall, it is clear that it is not a true fortified building, because of its large windows and blind corners. Continuing around the end of the chapel tower, you will see how it rises straight up out of the ditch, and it has quite large and formerly glazed windows on the upper floors. One of these retains its head of Caerbwdy stone.

Rounding the tower, the three windows of the chapel and the top storey of the tall porch behind come into view. Note how the pattern and size of the blocks of stonework change about halfway up the wall; a feature which reflects different phases of construction. Note also the putlog holes, the small square sockets in which the medieval wooden scaffolding was set. These stop halfway up the wall, implying that the later work was built from the inside.

The next octagonal tower rises from a flared base and contains the closets and latrines which served the apartments inside. There are no arrowslits on the front face, which suggests that defence was not a concern by this date. If you now look towards the gatehouse, you will clearly see from the straight joint that it was built up against an earlier tower, which has now largely collapsed. Three pieces of this tower lie within the ditch, with a latrine chute passing right through.

The chapel tower and the chapel — marked by the line of three large windows carved in purple Caerbwdy stone — from the exterior of the castle.

A TOUR OF THE BOROUGH OF LLAWHADEN

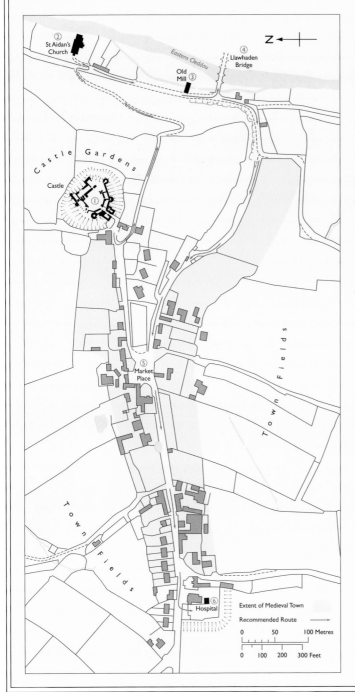

The borough of Llawhaden was founded by Bishop Bek very early in his episcopate, but the crucial step in its development was a grant of 1281 in which King Edward I gave licence for a weekly market and two annual three-day fairs. The fairs were held around the feasts of St Luke the Evangelist (18 October) and St Martin (11 November). It is, therefore, somewhat suprising that there is little in the present village of Llawhaden to suggest that it was once a bustling market town. However, there are sufficient clues surviving to give some idea of the former layout and these are revealed in a short walk around the village.

1 Castle — the castle was the centre of the bishop's power, and home of his constable who controlled the affairs of the borough.

2 St Aidan's Church — the church was a pre-Conquest foundation (see the carved cross at the east end), but the building with its unusual tower survives from the Middle Ages.

3 Old Mill — the present mill (a private house) is dated 1765, and stands on the site of the medieval mill, the rental from which contributed a major proportion of the borough income.

4 Llawhaden Bridge — the eighteenth-century bridge originally had five arches. The river has always had an important salmon and sea-trout fishery.

5 Market Place — the path leads up one of the former streets of the borough to the market place. The weekly market and twice-yearly fairs were the centre of the borough's economic activity.

6 Hospital — behind the community hall is a large, stone-vaulted building, part of a hospital for the poor and aged founded by Bishop Bek in 1287. It stood at the western end of the medieval borough and there are significant traces of a ditched enclosure surrounding the ruins.

The late medieval yeoman's house at Carswell stands amid farm buildings on a slight promontory overlooking the marshy valley of the Ritec.

CARSWELL MEDIEVAL HOUSE

A HISTORY OF THE HOUSE

Carswell farm stands on a slight promontory overlooking the valley of the Ritec. This marshy valley was originally a tidal creek opening on to the shore between Tenby and Penally some two miles (3.2km) to the east. In the Middle Ages, small boats were able to move up the creek, reaching St Florence, a mile (1.6km) to the west. Since the railway was built across its mouth, it has become a reedy swamp. The farm takes its name from a spring just below the yard, with the first element — *cars* — derived from the English *cress*, the Welsh *gors* or marsh.

The history of Carswell can be traced back to the early fourteenth century, to the time when it formed part of the estates of the earls of Pembroke. These estates were initially created after the Norman conquest of south-west Wales (including the later Pembrokeshire) in the late eleventh century. They were divided up among the earl's knights, who in turn owed him a duty of military service. Each knight then divided his estate between his bondsmen, and one of these probably held Carswell.

In the early documents the site is nearly always linked with Torre or Tarr — the adjacent farm to the west. In 1326, the joint rental of these holdings was 5s. per annum, and later documents show that each represented one tenth of a knight's fee. Each comprised one carucate (about 120 acres; 48.5ha) of land. In 1324, however, it was estimated that Torre was worth £1 6s. 8d. per annum — over ten times its annual rent. The earliest occupant who can actually be traced at Carswell is William Wyte, who witnessed a document of 1397 involving a transfer of land on the nearby Trefloyne estate.

At the end of the fourteenth century Carswell disappears from the records, until it is once again mentioned in a number of documents from the end of the reign of Queen Elizabeth (1558–1603). By 1586, the property had been divided in two, for in that year Richard Merydith of Pembroke sold his portion — a messuage (or house) and a garden on the hillside — to a merchant named Peter Williams. The other half appears to have been owned by the

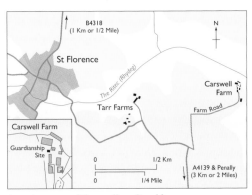

Location map of Carswell medieval house.

'*maior, bailyffs and burgesses of Tenby*', since in 1601 they let their land at Carswell to Thomas Bowen of Trefloyne. In 1689, the portion owned by the Williams family was bought by a number of local citizens for £290 10s., so that the rent could provide for the '*relief of the poor and aged of the towne of Tenbie*'.

From 1689, Carswell remained in the dual ownership of the trustees of the Tenby Charities and the rector of St Mary's Tenby until 1960, when the tenants purchased the whole farm. Carswell medieval house was placed in the care of the State in 1982 by the Thomas family of Carswell farm, and is now maintained by Cadw: Welsh Historic Monuments.

A DESCRIPTION OF THE HOUSE

To appreciate the character of this unusual building, it is best to walk around the outside first. Facing the gate into the small paddock is its eastern face, where the doorway to the first floor survives. Originally, it would have been approached by a flight of stone steps. Alongside the door, there is evidence for later modifications to the house — a crude addition with the sockets for its rafters surviving in the mortar.

Proceeding clockwise around the house, in the south face you will see the outline of three blocked windows — one on the ground floor and two above. The western side of the building is dominated by a massive stone chimney, which has projecting stone bands to throw off the

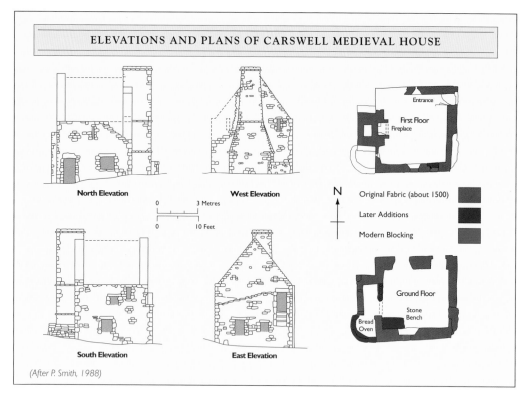

ELEVATIONS AND PLANS OF CARSWELL MEDIEVAL HOUSE

North Elevation   West Elevation

0   3 Metres
0   10 Feet

N

Entrance

First Floor
Fireplace

Original Fabric (about 1500)

Later Additions

Modern Blocking

Ground Floor

Stone Bench

Bread Oven

South Elevation   East Elevation

(After P. Smith, 1988)

rainwater. Unlike the well-known round 'Flemish' or 'Pembrokeshire' chimneys (of which there are good examples in the nearby village of St Florence) the Carswell chimney is square in section. A round bread oven, which would have had a slated or domed roof (now lost), has been added in one corner.

On the north side, one of the original slit windows in the first floor survives. Here, of the two entrances to the ground floor, that to the left with its simple dressed-stone surround is the original, the other is a later alteration. Inside, the ground-floor room or undercroft covered with a stone barrel vault probably functioned as a kitchen and living area. There was one small window to the south, which is now blocked, and there was another to the north, through which a doorway to a later extension was cut. The room is dominated by a huge fireplace with a low 'segmental' arch. There are remains of a later wall built to reduce the size of the opening, probably in the nineteenth century. Standing inside the fireplace, you can look up through the square chimney, and you will notice the reddened and blackened stones of the hearth, as well as the bread oven to one side. Adjacent to the fireplace is a stone bench or work table.

You should now leave the ground floor and climb the modern wooden staircase to the upper storey. From here, it is clear that the original doorway was hinged on the left-hand side, and the stone step was cut in a curve to allow it to open inwards. Traces of the hole for the wooden bolt can be found inside the jamb on the right-hand side. There was just one room at this level, probably intended to serve as the solar or private chamber of the family. It was lit by four narrow slit windows, set in deep embrasures, of which two remain. There is one to the left of the fireplace and a second in the northern side. The one on the southern side is blocked, and another has been lost in the collapse of the masonry alongside the fireplace. A further inserted window on the south (now blocked) suggests that later in its life this room may have been partitioned into two. The room was heated by a small but prominent fireplace with a stone hood carried on a curving lintel and plain corbels. The present floor is the top of the stone vault beneath, but originally this must have been covered with a surface of plaster or beaten clay. The roof of the building was steeply pitched and set behind the gables.

On leaving the house, although it is not open to the public, it is worth looking across the yard at another tall rectangular stone building, probably a second house. This too has a stone-vaulted ground storey, together with evidence for an entry at first-floor level from an external flight of steps.

THE DATING AND FUNCTION OF THE HOUSE

The documentary history of Carswell begins early in the fourteenth century when it was probably occupied by a yeoman farmer of some wealth. Although the house is built very solidly, it contains only two rooms. Various original features survive, but they are not highly decorated, and this makes close stylistic dating somewhat difficult. The windows are narrow and rectangular, and are set in deep embrasures; the doors have simple rectangular surrounds. These features suggest a possible sixteenth-century date rather than anything earlier.

The massive square chimney breast is found on other buildings, such as the Tudor merchant's house in Tenby which dates from the late fifteenth century, and other examples survive on seventeenth-century farmhouses. The first-floor fireplace is a simple version of a type common in medieval castles and halls. The stone-vaulted ground floor is found in many types of medieval Pembrokeshire buildings. Such vaults are well-known in churches, castles, fortified houses, merchants' town houses in Pembroke and Haverfordwest, and in a group of small rural

The house, seen from the south-west, is dominated by a massive stone chimney, though the remains of a later bread oven, now missing its roof, can be seen in the foreground. The projecting stone bands on the chimney served to throw off rainwater.

In common with Carswell, the so-called Tudor merchant's house in Tenby has a massive square chimney breast (Wales Tourist Board).

Late medieval buildings of similar construction to Carswell house can be found elsewhere in southern Pembrokeshire. Nearby West Tarr (above) is known to have had links with Carswell since 1324, while another small vaulted building survives at East Trewent Farm, Freshwater (below).

houses similar to Carswell. Vaults of this form can date back to the late twelfth century.

Unfortunately, archaeological excavation around the house at Carswell has not made the dating any clearer; the earliest finds belong to the sixteenth century. The unusual feature at Carswell is that there appear to be two houses, of similar form and date, so close to each other. This may reflect the break-up of the farm into two portions, which seems to have occurred sometime between the end of the fourteenth century and the first record of the division in 1586. All this evidence provides no more than a wide span of time in which to place the construction of Carswell. Nevertheless, a date of around 1500 seems the most likely.

The presence of a stone-vaulted ground level, with independent access to the first floor, has led to the suggestion that houses of this form were built for defensive purposes. This might be confirmed by some archaeological evidence of a walled precinct around the two Carswell houses, traces of which were noted in 1867 by the antiquarian Edward Barnwell (d. 1884). The plan and form of the houses at Carswell can be found elsewhere in southern Pembrokeshire. Indeed, a very similar building survives at nearby West Tarr farm, which has had links with Carswell since at least 1324. It differs in having a stone-vaulted upper storey as well as the ground floor, and with no fireplace in the lower level. West Tarr, however, is set against a steep hillslope and is in a very unlikely defensible position.

A little further afield are the small vaulted buildings at East Trewent Farm, Freshwater East, and Kington Farm, Pembroke. Neither of these has any fireplaces. A similar building, with two stories above an undercroft containing a kiln, survives amongst the great complex of ruins at Sister's House, Minwear, on the Eastern Cleddau. The form of some of these buildings, particularly those at East Trewent and Kingston Farm, resembles later granaries which are widespread in farmyards throughout south-west Wales.

Carswell medieval house represents one of a group of yeoman dwellings peculiar to southern Pembrokeshire. They probably belong in the main to the late Middle Ages, and because they were built so robustly in stone, a number of fine examples have survived comparatively unaltered to the present day.

CAREW CROSS

The Carew Cross is one of the most magnificent early Christian monuments in Wales, and is seen by many as a milestone of Welsh art. It stands more than 13 feet (4.2m) high, on a stone plinth situated alongside the main road through Carew village, and just inside the grounds of the well-known castle.

It is a so-called composite 'slab' cross, made of two pieces of different stone. The slab comprising the wheel-head and its neck is cut from Carboniferous sandstone, probably quarried in Carmarthenshire. This is tenoned into the tall shaft below, itself an igneous rock (a microtonalite), which outcrops in the Preseli mountains. All the faces are richly carved with panels of geometric or interwoven patterns, laboriously raised by pecking away the surrounding stone. Most of these designs were

Standing more than 13 feet (4.2m) high, the Carew Cross appears to have been erected either as a memorial to Maredudd ap Edwin (d. 1035), or perhaps to celebrate his kingship.

derived from a native stylistic heritage, though
Saxon and Viking influences were also
important in the development of art in Wales
at this time.

The western side of the cross is seen first.
Much of the decoration has flaked off the face
of the wheel-head over the centuries, and only
the lower arm showing part of a 'Stafford' knot
survives. The remainder of the decoration on
this side fills a series of panels. Immediately
below the wheel-head are two swastika-like
symbols, betraying an Irish influence. The
panel at the top of the shaft on this side, with
its plaitwork running through a line of rings, is
a characteristic Viking-age motif. Near the
centre of the shaft there is an inscribed panel
(see below), and there is a further panel of
plaitwork and a T-pattern at the base.

The opposite — eastern — face of the cross
has a different sequence of patterns, showing
some of the motifs visible on the other side
and introducing new ones. The lowest panel
consists of a bold eight-cord, double-beaded
plaitwork wrapped around circular pellets —
another Viking rather than a native device.

Each of the narrow side faces of the shaft
of the cross has a running plaited decoration.

THE INSCRIPTION

The inscription on the western face of the
Carew Cross has puzzled antiquarians for
more than two hundred years. Many variations
on the text and its meaning have been put
forward. As early as 1784, a correspondent
in the *Gentleman's Magazine* wrote about the
inscription, saying that 'the interpretation of
which from an ingenious gentleman will be
deemed a favour'. By far the most convincing
explanation was put forward by Dr C. A. R.
Radford in 1949. His reading of the inscription
was:

MARGIT
EUT.RE
X.ETG[UIN]. FILIUS

In translation this reads as:

[The Cross of] *Margiteut* [Maredudd]
son of Etguin [Edwin]

*A detail of the panel on the western face of the
cross, inscribed in memory of Maredudd ap Edwin.*

Maredudd ap Edwin was a descendant of
the celebrated legislator, Hywel Dda (Hywel the
Good, d. 949/50), whose name provided the
focus for the medieval laws of Wales. In 1033,
Maredudd became joint ruler of Deheubarth —
the kingship covering south-west Wales — with
his brother Hywel. Two years later, he was
killed in battle by the sons of Cynan. Hence,
the Carew Cross, erected either as a memorial
to Maredudd, or to celebrate his kingship, must
have been carved between 1033 and 1035. The
blank panel alongside the inscription was clearly
meant for another epigraph; perhaps it was
intended for Hywel who died in 1044. Yet it is
puzzling that the inscription should be so cryptic
and difficult to decipher. Most pre-Conquest
crosses with inscriptions are clearly and boldly
cut, so that the few literate people of the time
could have read or spoken out their content.
The patron of this large and expensive cross
would surely have intended that his name
would be remembered.

The Carew Cross represents the culmination
in the development of the early Christian (pre-
Conquest) monuments of Wales. It is one of only
four examples of this composite or two-piece
type surviving in the Principality, all of which
must have been closely linked. Just as large and
as highly decorated is the cross in St Brynach's
churchyard at Nevern. This has many similarities
with Carew. Its shaft is apparently of the same
igneous stone as that at Carew, with the head
carved from a coarser sandstone. A number of
decorative motifs are shared by both crosses,
and the Nevern shaft has two inscribed panels,
each of which has proved impossible to decipher.
It is indeed tempting to see both the Carew
and Nevern crosses as the work of the same
craftsman.

The less complete examples of composite crosses are the 'Samson Cross' at Llantwit Major (Vale of Glamorgan), and another from Llanfynydd (Carmarthenshire) — clearly inscribed 'Eiudon' — now in the National Museum & Gallery, Cardiff. There are indications that the 'Samson Cross' at one time bore traces of original painting, and there is other evidence that tenth- and eleventh-century crosses were highly painted and their patterns picked out in rich colours. This may have been true of the Carew Cross, giving it a more robust and vivid appearance.

Though very large and highly carved, the cross is not as fine as some of the contemporary examples in Ireland or Cumbria. The shaft, for instance, has a slightly sinuous profile and steps in on its eastern side. The wheel-head sits rather awkwardly on the shaft, and the proportions are not entirely satisfying. As the cross is made of two different types of stone, from distant sources, it is possible that the two parts of the monument were fashioned close to their quarries and finally put together at the memorial site. None the less, the mixture of 'native' Welsh, Irish and Viking motifs in the decoration emphasizes the importance of maritime links in this area in both pre-Conquest and earlier times.

Although the head is missing, there is a further shaft of a composite cross surviving in the parish church at Llantwit Major. It is known as the 'Samson Cross' and perhaps commemorates a local ruler or religious leader (Wales Tourist Board).

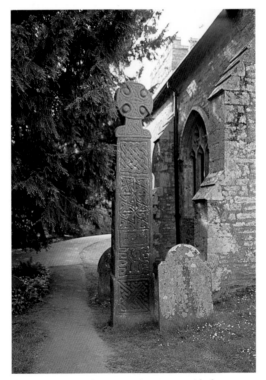

Carew is a composite or two-piece cross, with the head tenoned into the shaft below. Further north at St Brynach's churchyard in Nevern, there is another fine example of the same form of cross, which shares several of the decorative motifs seen at Carew, and may represent the work of the same craftsman.

LATER HISTORY OF THE CROSS

The Carew Cross once stood further out into the road, which is an unusual position for a cross of this type and date. However, we know from recent archaeological excavations undertaken at Carew that the castle was built over a heavily defended stronghold raised by one of the native Welsh chieftains of early Christian Deheubarth. Perhaps the cross stood within this stronghold, and was moved by one of the great medieval or Tudor lords of Carew, adding to the grandeur of the approach through a line of courts to the heart of the castle. Moreover, the cross would no doubt have served to reaffirm the links of these lords with the early princes of Deheubarth. If so, it may have been brought from a local churchyard, most likely that at nearby Carew Cheriton.

The cross was first recorded around 1690 by the antiquarian, Edward Lhwyd (d. 1709). A copy of his rather clumsy sketch of the west

In 1941, the Carew Cross was dismantled and placed in safe storage for the duration of the Second World War.

side still survives. It implies that the wheel-head had lost its decoration on this side by that date.

The level of the road was lowered in 1822, when a stone plinth was constructed around the base of the cross. In 1844, the wheel-head was reported as leaning heavily at an angle of 45 degrees, and it was reset using lead from the Norman font at the church. By 1869, bill-stickers were using the cross for their advertisements, and there was a complaint that periodically it had to be cleaned. Also during the Victorian period, the inscription on the cross was copied on two stones near Fethard Castle (Waterford), in Ireland. About this time, the Ordnance Survey added a new motif of their own, a bench mark at the base of the eastern face.

Carew Cross was placed in the care of the Office of Works by the Honourable Mrs Trollope in 1923, when it was moved a few feet off the road to its present position. The cross is now maintained by Cadw: Welsh Historic Monuments.

FURTHER READING

Lamphey Bishop's Palace and Llawhaden Castle

J. Wyn Evans and Rick Turner, *St Davids Bishop's Palace — St Non's Chapel* (Cadw, Cardiff 1999).

Richard Fenton, *A Historical Tour Through Pembrokeshire* (London 1811); reprinted (Brecon 1903).

Brian Howells, *Medieval Lamphey* (Lamphey).

Brian Howells (editor) *Pembrokeshire County History, III, Early Modern Pembrokeshire, 1536–1815* (Haverfordwest 1987).

R. F. Isaacson (editor) and R. Arthur Roberts, *The Episcopal Registers of St. David's 1397 to 1518*, 3 volumes (Cymmrodorion Record Series, **6**, London 1917–20).

C. A. Ralegh Radford, 'The Palace of the Bishops of St. Davids at Lamphey, Pembrokeshire', *Archaeologia Cambrensis*, **93** (1938), 1–14.

C. A. Ralegh Radford, *Llawhaden Castle*, reprinted (HMSO, Cardiff 1980).

M. W. Thompson, *The Decline of the Castle* (Cambridge 1988).

Michael Thompson, *Medieval Bishops' Houses in England and Wales* (Aldershot 1998).

J. W. Willis-Bund (editor) *The Black Book of Saint David's* (Cymmrodorion Record Series, **5**, London 1902).

Carswell Medieval House

E. L. Barnwell, 'Domestic Architecture of South Pembrokeshire', *Archaeologia Cambrensis*, third series, **13** (1867), 193–204, 363–74; **14** (1868), 70–84.

Edward Laws, *The History of Little England Beyond Wales* (London 1888); reprinted (Haverfordwest 1995).

Peter Smith, *Houses of the Welsh Countryside*, 2nd edition (London 1988).

Carew Cross

V. E. Nash-Williams, *The Early Christian Monuments of Wales* (Cardiff 1950).

Mark Redknap, *The Christian Celts: Treasures of Late Celtic Wales* (Cardiff 1991).

William George Spurrell, *The History of Carew* (Carmarthen 1921).